Everest and Chips

by Robert Hull

with illustrations by
Matt Kenyon

OXFORD

UNIVERSITY PRESS

Great Clarendon Street, Oxford OX2 6DP

Oxford University Press is a department of the University of Oxford.
It furthers the University's objective of excellence in research, scholarship,
and education by publishing worldwide in

Oxford New York

Auckland Bangkok Buenos Aires
Cape Town Chennai Dar es Salaam Delhi Hong Kong Istanbul
Karachi Kolkata Kuala Lumpur Madrid Melbourne Mexico City Mumbai
Nairobi São Paulo Shanghai Taipei Tokyo Toronto

Oxford is a registered trade mark of Oxford University Press
in the UK and in certain other countries

British Library Cataloguing in Publication Data available

ISBN 0-19-276309-1

3 5 7 9 10 8 6 4

Typeset by Mary Tudge (Typesetting Services)
Designed by Jo Samways
Printed and bound in Great Britain
by Cox & Wyman Ltd

Contents

A. Non

If you're anon
you can be no one

so no one knows
that was your poem

or bit of prose
and you're free to say

when it's fallen flat
—with a silent splat—

'Oh yes, a cousin
of my neighbour's

sister's vet
did that.'

Scientists Have Found

the hole in the ozone layer
is getting larger

which seems inevitable
considering how

holes in fences
holes in pockets
holes in socks
holes in your ideas

all get larger

Questions of Gravity

When I asked Dad
when he dropped his drink on the plane
why didn't it fall backwards?
he said he didn't know.

When I asked Dad
why does smoke go straight up
in the air? he said
he'd look it up.

When I asked Dad
on the moon would he weigh more
than on earth or less? he said
he wasn't sure.

My dad didn't know the answer
to any of these questions
which I think is surprising
because

he's been on the earth a long time
dropping things
smoking
and weighing a lot.

From Trees We Get

old ships
news
chairs
geography books
poems

as well as

huge clearings
power-saws
smoke-haze
empty homes.

If we're lucky
we also get from trees

the din of birds
forest floors
autumns
heavy mists
paths
the bark of deer
shadow.

And from trees we might even get
if we go on being lucky
really lucky

more trees.

Eclipse

It comes on inevitably
as calculated
but strangely it's a surprise too
though you can set your watch
to what's going to happen
as you start to slide beneath it

it happens the same as ever
the air growing fearful
light decaying
the world losing interest in itself

nothing is as it was
the barn isn't well
the sun's losing control
the grass has dark longings

an immense pallor
a sickness such as the moon
has never known
infects the earth
drains the life of fields houses
the river clouds

at the centre
only a shadowy place
where you stand
in a swirl of cold
which is all the world

you hardly speak
or touch or look at anything
except to be witness
to confirm what's happening

for the moment
this is the only
experience there is

till only slowly
but as inevitably
as calculated
dark changes its mind
the sentence is lifted

in four or five minutes
the fields recover their breath
the roof fence the outbuildings
become strong again
shadows lose their anxiety

and finally reprieved
the day walks free

the sun rediscovers
swallows on the river

out of pawn
the crow's feathers gleam

it's over
you can leave
make plans
live again.

Riddle

I eat razor-blades
read prices
sing.

I give you your sight back
and lead planes by the nose.

I'm a healer
who shatters diamonds
a reader
who burns books.

Laser

Freedom . . .

'Miss, can I carry on reading this book?'

'Well, you can for a minute,
then you must get on
with your Freedom Project.'

Dictionary

How nice to be
a dictionary—
complete
concise
authentic,

full of words
like erudite
orate
replete
argentic—

replete with meaning
full of life
exhaustive
true
eccentric.

How nice to have
a million words
handy
when
you're writing,

a million words
that wait for you
and only
need
inviting—

you fish for words—
you cast around—
look,
they're already
biting!

English Rules Not OK

Rule 1—'Don't use a preposition at the end of a sentence'

The trouble is
that as long as jokes are laughed at
and chewing gum's stuck under
and parents are got round

as long as washing up's got out of
and shoulders are leaned on
and dog-dirt's stepped in

as long as socks have holes in
and holes are what rabbits disappear down

sentences that prepositions come at the end of
and sentences that prepositions shouldn't come at the end of

will be what life is full of.

Rule 2—'Find another word instead of *nice*'

But *nice* is a nice word,
one of the nicest if you ask me.

Reliable people are nice,
best friends are nice—most of the time.
Kindness is nice, and hamsters,
some teachers, and all ice-cream.

And coming home tired and getting your favourite meal
in front of television when you don't have to rack
your brain for ideas for a story for homework
or try to think up more words instead of the nice ones
you already thought of is

really nice.

Rule 3—'Don't use *and* all the time'

But I like *and*
I'm a fan.

Without *and*
where would here and now be
and yes and no
and you and me?

Without *and*
the knife wouldn't have a fork to eat with
and the burger would have had its chips.

And adds to life
it's a more-of-where-that-came-from,
a sunny plus,
not a misty minus.

And and and
keeps stories chugging along
like a little engine.

Without *and*
no one could be the life and soul of the party
the bible would collapse
and the egg couldn't bring home the bacon.

Ripe conkers are *and*
and second helpings
and extra time

And big sloppy dogs
and daft jokes
and love
and the genius you'll be tomorrow.

And . . .

Dictionary Entry

Slutch—

was what we chucked
around in handfuls,
or crawled out
of ditches covered in,
it was what we got
slutched up with.

Not
farmer's *muck*
or mum's *dirt* or *mud*,
certainly not bible *mire*,

no, the liquidy stuff belly-flop
saves got made in,
and sucked-off clogs got
pulled from—

slutch.

Countrysiders' Code

Please do not leave your rubbish in the country

Please take away
your rusty defunct tractors
harrows, bailers, and seeders
your piled tyres, emptied fertilizer bags
shell-cases and clay-pigeon remains

Please leave the countryside
as you would wish to find it,
please do not
remove this hedge
tranquillize those pheasants
pretend that isn't a footpath
herbicide those wildflowers

Please ensure
that your megatractors don't churn verges
that your ditches don't run grunge
that your business plans include birds
that your grass includes flowers

Please remember
who owns bloom and scent and song
and who needs silent fields and fenced-off rivers
and whose countryside it is
and whose future it is

Exercise Biker

The scenery's a wall,
I'm getting nowhere at all

with this thing you can't
read write or think on,

this trendy treadmill
for the gaunt and thin

to get gaunter and thinner on,
that's called a bike

though the amount of uphill
and down dale it does is nil.

So it's for sale, my stylish,
solid, Swedish

waste of cash—
no mark, no damage,

remarkably low mileage,
only one

careful owner
who from now on

intends going nowhere
his own way.

Mr T. Huxley Discovers Dinner

Mr Huxley at Christmas dinner
taking apart a bird
took a long look at some bones
spoke not a word

and took himself off to the fossils
in his office.
When he returned he said:
'We are astounded to notice

the bones of this bird
set before us
resemble those
of Megalosaurus.'

The cooling
Christmas dish
got gradually less
and less more-ish

as Mr Huxley continued:
'It is not a wild hypothesis
to suggest that the phylum
of the whole class Aves

has its roots
in dinosaurian reptiles.'
As he said this probably
he was all smiles,

because it's not every year
you think you discover
the distant dinosaur
is Christmas dinner undercover.

It's Christmas so . . .

Rudolf the Red-nose
Reindeer muzaks through

the department store
right into the loo.

But out in the street
the sun shines bright

on the glinting brass
of a cheery group

playing Good
King Wenceslas.

It lights up red and white
bobble-hats

and glistens a bit
on dribble and spit

as the cornet sings
each fine old tune

and the trombone
glides deep

and crisp and even
and the quietly treading

tuba pumps its
yes and yes

in gentle oompahs.
They stop for mince pies

and the biggest size
helping of pud

you ever could,
then slap themselves

warm with a one
two We Three Kings

of Orient Are
off again pouring

hard-blown breath
up into the sunshine,

as Hark the Herald
Angels Sing

like anything
and people stand

amid December's
not much snow

while others go gathering
winter fuel

stamps, presents etc
or come forward to give

thanks for the true jazz
of Christmas.

Peace Process

Things are finally moving,
a spokesperson says.

Even now officials
are on their knees measuring

the huge handshake
the leaders did up there,

while specialists scrutinize
the innards of smiles.

It appears the leaders
may have been alone long enough

to consummate a sentence,
which could mean that the people

may yet be permitted
not to run out of future.

Making Men and Women—
a Maya story from Central America

And the Creator and Maker
said to the birds and four-footed animals:
'Sing, praise us, speak, give thanks to us
for making you.'

But the birds, pumas, snakes, jaguars, and deer
could only hiss, or snarl, or bark, or warble—
they could not form words of praise.

So the Creator and Maker said,
'We shall make others who will praise us obediently
and sing beautiful hymns and adore us.'

And they shaped a creature of mud and water.
It spoke—but it hadn't enough thought,
and lacked the strength to stand; it slipped
and slumped about and was useless
so they destroyed it.

And the Creator and Maker tried again and shaped creatures
of wood. And the wood beings talked, and looked human,
and had children of wood who talked and looked human.
But these people of wood had no souls,
and no feelings or expression, no laughter or tears.

And to get rid of them the Creator and Maker
sent black skies and a flood, and everyone starved.
The village animals had no food. The dogs and cattle
took sticks and began to beat the wood people
to drive them away. The pots and pans of the houses joined in:
'You hurt us and broke us and burnt us,
scalded us, blackened us!'
When the wood people climbed up the walls to escape
the walls leaned and hurled them down to the ground.

And so the wood people were beaten
and driven out of their villages to the woods
and forests; there they turned into monkeys—
monkeys look like humans because once
they were wood people.

And the Creator and Maker tried again, this time
with yellow and white corn. And they were successful—
these new creatures had good figures, they walked and talked
and thought with great intelligence. Their knowledge was huge,
they could see all the world clearly, and watched it like gods.

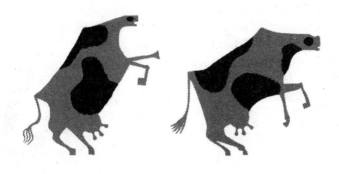

And the Creator and Maker agreed
that these new beings saw too clearly.
'Their sight reaches into everything,
they understand all they can see.
They will be like gods. They will be too proud
to honour and praise us.'

And the Creator and Maker took flints of obsidian
and chipped at the clear surface of their gaze,
and blew mist into their eyes and clouded them over
so they saw the world as if in a misted-up mirror.

So at the beginning of time, the first clear wisdom
of men and women was taken from them,
and their understanding was dimmed for ever.

Leaving

My binoculars
can't locate the plane

you're out in space in
gliding amongst the stars

at the end of the garden
somewhere in Orion.

His dark sword-belt
glitters in the poplars,

empty and bare
of leaves in winter

as this house is now
without you.

Riddles

It sings gently
as it fills the willows
with flowing white.

The flowers have to agree
with everything it does.

Wind

An empty grin
lit from within.
Yo-yo-ing
shadows of teeth
in a moon of mouth.

Hallowe'en
Pumpkin

Arundel Swimming Pool

is good fun
for everyone—

teetery toddlers
bald dawdlers
and ancient waddlers
keen lean chaps
in goggles and skull-caps
counting the laps—

it's great
for two-yard dashers
unnecessary splashers
crawlers sprawlers
screamers dreamers
bare-back riders
sun-lotioned idlers
backwards-down-the-sliders
drop-outs on loungers
tiny ice-cream scroungers—

it's so smashing for everyone
with all the slosh
and swirl and splash
and shouting friendly din
and the view of the castle
and blue sky now and again
and clouds and swallows and martins
skimming in—

they're going to close it
and turn it into an *Important*
perhaps *Significant*
possibly *Exclusive and Prestigious*
or even *Significantly and Prestigiously Exclusive*

DEVELOPMENT

and instead of an old swimming pool
which is only good fun for everyone
they'll have something to make a lot of money
for someone.

Everest and Chips

There was once a painter
who liked chips so much
he put them in all his paintings

His paintings were called

Forest Dawn and Chips
Gondolas at Rest and Chips
Everest and Chips
Rain Steam Speed and Chips
The Death of Ophelia and Chips
Bandaged Ear and Chips
Chicken and Chips
and so on

When he sold his paintings
he always added 70p
to cover his chip expenses

What's What

what's patient
is mums
what hurries
is thumbs

what squiggles
is toes
what squabbles
is no's

what dangles
is cuffs
what cuddles
is muffs

what's dribbly
is noses
what's likely
is dozes

what's cuddly
is bears
what's wobbly
is chairs

what rumbles
is tums
what grumbles
is mums

Classic Rail Journey

Welcome to our classic crumbling station.
Your journey on one of our classically clapped-out trains
will begin here.

We hope.

It will start with a classic piece of misinformation
on our classically fuzzy speaker system
about the train now standing at Platform 1.

The train now standing at Platform 1
classically enough
isn't,
and has just gone.

Equally classically,
there's no other train in sight.

We now have as expected
an unexpected short delay
followed by a special classic announcement
saying the train due to arrive on Platform 2 will appear
even later than was apologized for earlier
due to classic signal failure.

We shall try to ensure that our classic apologies saying
your train is not on time
are frequent
and on time.

Because classically we also have no crew
at the station further up the line.

May we inform you
there is nothing for you to do
but wait in our classically crumby bar
and have a coffee classic
served with the classic
There you go.

If only
we did.

Taxi!

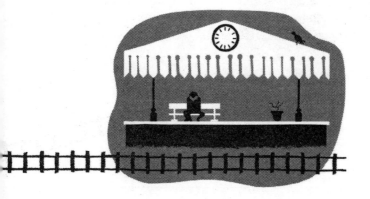

Parents are Funny Sometimes

Mum and Dad go dead polite
whenever they invite
their posh friends round.

When the dog lets off
they cough.

Absence Note

Dear Mrs James,
I've desided to keep mum at home today.
School and everything's getting her down,
she's got parent burnout, it's all got too much,
what with as well as takeing me and Ed
and Danny and Jane next door in every day
and bringing us home, Tuesdays
she collects me after my guitarrh lesson
and waits while Danny has maths coatching
round Mr Fellows' house then Wedensdays
is my football practise plus a lift
to evening rehersals for Ed for Cats
in the village hall. Thurdays after school
is extra tests for Sats for me, and Fridays
before school it's speling club which dad says
I have to go to I don't see why. Saturday morning
their's football a match and Saturday afternoon
we go family shopping. So I rung up the docter
and asked can she give mum some rest pills
or something but she says to take her out for lunch
on the bus with money from dad and go shopping
for clothes or something and get some flowers
and keep her away from the car which is what
we're doing. So I'm not coming into school today
or tomorrow probably because this is inportant
I know youll agree and be simperthetic,
take care, see you Monday, love,
Melissa.

Punct. ex.

. . . .
spawn
spores
score-book no-scores
acupunctures
bike punctures

rook-nests
holes in vests
eyelets

lobs
blobs
spots
i-dots
belly-fuls
tennis-balls

plodder's pauses

, , , , , , ,
useful hooks
to hang in space

distant birds
frayed ends of anything

tiny dark thoughts
to give pause

motes
dark stars
tadpoles turning left

" " " "
dizzy
bi-focal
seeing two of everything
sociable

couples
confederates
perfectly matched dates

confetti

close markers
cartoon eyes in the dark
pairs of tent-pegs
fish and shadow

twin slits
kites
thin lines mating

! ! ! ! ! ! !
cor struth
not on your life
that's my wife
feelings getting warmer
careful round the corner
drunken snooker
look out
shout
full-stop with a sprout
something hot
line plus a dot
plant in a pot

CAPITAL
very upper
jolly good
snooty
IMpOrtant
Headmasters
quite so

: : : : : :
dominoes
dice
twice
holes in foolscap
drunk fullstops
eyes lying down

* * *

splats
cow-pats
remains of straw hats

snowflakes
places where it aches

cracks in ice
glints in binoculars
broken wing-mirrors
Mars and others
gold stars

In This Dream

I'm explaining the difference
between fichu and fondue

and fu-fu and frou-frou,
when someone in a tu-tu

says why not try some tiramisu
it'll amuse you,

I say I'd sooner samba like in the Congo
or rumba to drums say bongo

but she's Swiss and prefers to judo and yodel
with yoga and some strudel,

and tells me it's bogus
to go tangoing round Alpine meadows in togas,

I say why don't we ramble and doodle
cavort and canoodle

and she says you old humbug
you step out like a Struldbrug,

so what we have is frivolous chat,
and at the drop of a hat

discuss serious issues
like fissures in tissues

and whether snowshoes in igloos
cause Inuit to-dos

and if you should ever take aspirins
while sewing on sequins

and do poodles need hairdos
and does Corfu have cuckoos

and why do some people with brains of papier mâché
have so much social cachet

and why are funny dreams so confusing
and not really amusing?

Molto Interesting Half-time Pep Talk
[*an Italian manager in the Premiership had his half-time talk translated into English*]

Verdi 'ell 'e come from to score the first?
it was a pizza cake you give them and the second too
ok so you can't help the free-kick canaletto off you in the net
anyway the ref doing us no per favore chianti see the big elbow?
I go tagliatelli'm but his brain playing libero
but this half we 'ave to pasta the ball quicker out of defence
or we get salamied
and when we got the ball lasagne on to it for heaven's sake
this half the midfield got to prosciutto further forward
and no minestrone more chances
the crowd haven't siena a thing yet
remember we need a risotto or we're out
their forwards not espresso enough to hurt us
and the big one took a gnocchi on the break
and no red cards don't get into any cheap frascatis ok?

Snowdrops

The pony-tailed game-keeper strolls from his truck,
SS's in damson chevrons tattooed on his cheek—
'It's private, mate.'

I don't say it,
but I've come to this river
in frost, flood, and drought
for twenty-odd years, to watch
its martins and fieldfares,
its snipe, and toads, and voles,

and the snowdrops
that assemble in mid-January in thousands
along the sandy stream under the alders.

'It's the landowner, not me.
I wouldn't bother. He gets mad
when people don't keep to the path.'

'Mad' seems to tell me something—
and the easy way he's pretending
he's not really carrying a gun
loaded or unloaded over his arm.

I'm learning that any mercenary
helping an owner say 'mine'
with SS's tattooed in chevrons on his face
and a gun at ease on his arm
needs agreeing with.

So in deference to the landowner
who's started to own the river
and the old broken bridge over it,
as well as the abandoned railway,
the herons, the snipe, the snowdrops,
and now the sudden rain and probably
the clouds it's strayed from—
I retreat.

Today I'm playing the game
of helping the landowner
keep heron and water,
snipe and snowdrop in order,
and tomorrow
—if it's not raining—
I'm coming back.

This Building is Alarmed . . .

the revolving door can't stop
the mirrors are in two minds
the fluorescent lighting has a tic
the CCTV's swaying its head from side to side
the chandelier's trembling
the lounge-chairs are paralysed
the carpet is backing up
the wind is moaning on the stairs
the lift has turned claustrophobic
the knives in the drawer feel trapped

this building is alarmed . . .

Riddles

Daily I tear up hair
riding down into valleys
sailing over skinny hills
slashing jagged jungles.

Razor

We study feet from close up.
We each perform our work differently,
not knowing what the other is doing.
We both have a firm grasp of our subject.

Socks

Having Eaten Too Much

I went to the Leisure Centre
Tone Zone

a sort of hone-your-own
when it's overblown
flesh and bone zone

with a go-it-alone
on machinery zone
where you pick your own
push pull heave thrust pedal

path to a personal
groan zone.

But

feeling suddenly funny
in the hip-
bone-zone

I decided to postpone
considerations of tone
and return to the leisurely-
working-from-home-
on-the-phone zone

though

via the Centre's hot coffee tea
chocolate apple-pie scone
and ice-cream-
cone zone

where
wrestling with a thought
lifting a heavy doughnut
I tried to work out
how you build up
such a powerful appetite

in the healthy-impulse-that's-
suddenly-flown zone.

The Girl Who Made the Stars—
a Bushman story

The girl arose,
she put her hands into the wood ashes
and she said to them:
'Wood ashes
you must become the Milky Way
and lie along the sky
and go round with the stars
standing nicely round.'

And the girl threw the wood ashes up into the sky
and they became the Milky Way.

And the Milky Way gently glows
feeling that it is wood ashes

strewn along the sky
going round with the stars.

Beginnings

Perhaps all this

was shouted into being
by the sudden anger
of thunder

or sky
whet her fingers
in sprawled lakes
and sang the winds
across a flute

or the tree
of dark fell
and levered out
a root-face of white rock

or a frog
climbed to the top
of the pond of dark
and gulped out light

or from the wall
of silence
trailed shining
cranesbill

or the newt
hiding dawn
under its belly
banked upwards
with spread hands

or a thrush
broke open the shell
where light coiled

or all of this
this morning.

Plastered

It's an inconvenience
having a split index finger
with a plaster on.

It gets harder
to phone the right person quickly
wash accurately
count out money.

It's like having another thumb
to consider but clumsier—
that juts out and butts in
and pops from under.

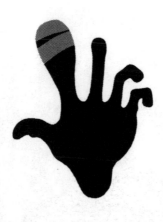

Thank goodness I'm not
a professional guitar-
or flute-player or embroiderer
or watch-fixer,
it's awkward enough
pulling gloves on,
peeling carrots,
chopping wood,
pressing remotes
and so on,
and as for attending to letters
which means handling stamps
and sellotape and licking envelopes
and all that
for the time being I give up.

And I can't get my wallet
out of my back pocket
without difficulty . . .

Come to think of it,
in some ways . . .

Do not write poems about your father's death

the well-known poet said,
and especially not also several other kinds of poem
of the sort I try to write.

And as I took the bus home
—wondering was the driver's dad dead—
I thought what is it all about,
this influential advice dripping on my page,
this top-writer talk tippexing out
things I've thought?

Well what it is, I decided,
is groan-up literary readers
who've been to the university
a lot not to mention poetry readings
deciding we ought to write about
capital I Important Things—Wars, Plagues,
Famines, the Environment, the Millennium

etc not just frogs and tadpoles,
ailing hamsters, bawling babies,
football, old buses, bats, birds,
Tom and Jerry cartoons, cornflakes,
bad refs, sudden deaths, and all
the other un-

Important things I'll go on writing about
including bus-drivers whose dads
might be alive

and snotty poets.

Sound Count Down

turn of a tap
clicking cap

pulled plug
clinked mug

slowing trickle
final gurgle

squirt of spray
towel put away

cupboard door squeak
basket creak

something picked off the floor
opening door—

can it be
the bathroom's free?

What to do with two multi-coloured umbrellas

Open them out and swirl them round you
parachute with them off the bench
float them at the edge of the pond
fish up sticks with them
prod a brother
have a fast-flapping competition
sink one in a shallow part
tell a dad to rescue it
ask a dad to rescue it
twirl them fast in the water
get wet shaking them dry
put them up because suddenly it's sunny
leave them under a bench and go to the swings
nearly forget about them
go back to find them because it's started drizzling
put them up because it's raining hard.

Watch big drops of rain hit the pond
making ripple-circles like small
multi-coloured umbrellas opening.

Things with Feathers

'Hope' is the thing with feathers
That perches in the soul—Emily Dickinson

Give us a tune, thing with feathers—
sing it in all weathers.

Sing it for eagle, osprey, wren,
kite, owl, moorhen,

and all those feathered others—
cousins, sisters, brothers—

who share with us here
our precarious atmosphere,

beating its thinness till it rings
with their songs and wings.

Sing for each threatened kind
that's nested here time out of mind—

sing for the sapphire blur
of the kingfisher,

for the thrush who once lorded it
on our chestnut summit,

for the fewer sparrows brawling
under eaves and awnings,

for the bullfinch with the furnace
of chest who's forsaken us,

for the grebe with the fish-hook
in its half-shut beak,

for fading lapwing and lark,
and silenced corn-crake.

Sing against birdsong's
sad diminishing.

Let that be your tune,
thing with feathers.

Sing it in all weathers.

Space

On a sphere of blue
marbled with white
taking a trip
through silent night,

out for a spin
in starry space
go me and you
and the human race.